CCRA – CERTIFIED CREDIT RESEARCH ANALYST (LEVEL 2) EXAM PRACTICE QUESTIONS & DUMPS

EXAM STUDY GUIDE FOR CCRA LEVEL-2 (AIWMI) Exam Prep LATEST VERSION

Presented By: Quantic Books

About Quantic Books:

Quantic Books is a publishing house based in Princeton, New Jersey, USA. , a platform that is accessible online as well as locally, which gives power to educational content, erudite collection, poetry & many other book genres. We make it easy for writers & authors to get their books designed, published, promoted, and sell professionally on worldwide scale with eBook + Print distribution. Quantic Books is now distributing books worldwide.

Note: Find answers of the questions at the last of the book.

QUESTION 1

Case Facts as on March 31, 2012

Mark Construction Company (MCC) obtained an agreement for construction of a huge dam and hydro power project on river Shivna in Madhya Pradesh (MP). The project is of significance from the irrigation perception because of its location and according to the contract MCC will have to start construction of web of canals, reach road to dam, power house and other auxiliary components. MCC is supported by Mr. Thomas Mark, member of parliament of a leading party which in recent times established government in MP. Traditionally, MCC has been involved with construction of rural roads, small bridges and railway stands on agreement basis for the Government. MCC will have a separate special purpose vehicle (SPV) presented for this project.

The hydro power project undergoes the public private partnership arrangement of the Government of MP, consequently the private partner builds owns operates and transfers (BOOT) the hydro power plant. The full requisites of the hydro power project contract are given below:

1. The production of the dam, canals and hydro power plant must be started by the contractor. The Government of MP will attain land which will submerge on creation of dam and must acclimatize the proprietors of land.

2. MCC must have right to run the hydro power project from date of commencement of commercial operations (DCCO) for a period of 20 years and must transfer the task to Government afterward. More, SPV must be tax released for a period of five years from DCCO viz. FY17-FY21.

3. The power project is of 600 megawatts (MW) must comprise 4 units of 150 MW each. The anticipated cost of project is approximately INR3, 500 Million to be spent over a period of 4 year(s) the project is anticipated to be commercially operational by April 1, 2016 with two units operational on same day and one unit each will be operational on April 1, 2017 and April 1, 2018.

4. Means of finance:

Means of Finance	INR Million
Government Aid (To be classified as Equity)	500
Equity	900
Debt	2100

Means of Finance INR Million
Government Aid (To be categorized as Equity) 500Equity 900

Cost of Project	INR Million	Debt	Funding Govt Aid	Equity	Total
FY13 (April to march)	700	0	250	450	700
FY14	1200	500	250	450	1200
FY15	1200	1200	-		1200
FY15	400	400	-		400

Debt 2100

5. Amount if expenses anticipated in various years is given below:

Debt must bear a fixed rate of interest of 10% and all interest till DCCO must be added to the principal. The anticipated principal beside with capitalized interest is anticipated to be INR2, 400 Million (viz.INR2100 Million debt plus INR300 Million capitalized interest). The reimbursement of the same must be in 12 equated yearly installments starting from FY17.

Short projections for the period of FY17 to FY21 are given

Particular	FY17	FY18	FY19	FY20	FY21
Revenue from Power sale	600	900	1200	1320	1452
EBITDA %	72%	68%	65%	60%	60%
Interest Cost	240.00	220.00	200.00	180.00	160.00
Depreciation	175.00	175.00	175.00	175.00	175.00
PAT	17.00	217.00	405.00	437.00	536.20

below:

Progresses as on March 31, 2015

The project manager for the SPV made given comments at a question and answer session on March 31, 2015:

Since everyone know, we were running bang on schedule till we last encountered on December 21, 2014. From this day we are just left with one more year to finish the task early enough. Still, the flash floods which effected our dam site on this March 15, 2015 have made chaos in the district. I must not emphasize the loss of lives in the district since everyone knows about that. Our project has also been seriously hit because of the same and we have been measuring the damage over the last one week. After examining damage, we have made changes in project schedule. Now we will be making just only one unit of 150 MW operational on April 1, 2016 and 1 unit each will be added in each of succeeding year(s).

Development as on September 30, 2015
Post the flash floods, lot of environmentalists started raising issues of changes in environment because of construction of huge number of dams. A few Public Interest Litigations (PILs) have been filed in various courts.

Honorable High Court of MP on September 27, 2015, restricted construction of any dams in the district and restricted authorizations for new dams till next hearing scheduled on November 30, 2015. MCC in its bulletin has specified that they will apply to the higher court on the issue.

As a credit expert on March 31, 2012, which of the given sets of dangers are you going to put in your credit assessment note?

A. Off-take danger, Cost and Time over run danger, absence of management capability in such big projects.
B. Absence of management capability in huge projects, Exchange rate dangers, Cost and time over run dangers.
C. Cost and Time over run danger, absence of management capability in such big projects.
D. Outdated technology danger, political dangers and Cost and time over run dangers

QUESTION 2

Case Facts as on March 31, 2012

Mark Construction Company (MCC) obtained an agreement for construction of a huge dam and hydro power project on river Shivna in Madhya Pradesh (MP). The project is of significance from the irrigation perception because of its location and according to the contract MCC will have to start construction of web of canals, reach road to dam, power house and other auxiliary components. MCC is supported by Mr. Thomas Mark, member of parliament of a leading party which in recent times established government in MP. Traditionally, MCC has been involved with construction of rural roads, small bridges and railway stands on agreement basis for the Government. MCC will have a separate special purpose vehicle (SPV) presented for this project.

The hydro power project undergoes the public private partnership arrangement of the Government of MP, consequently the private partner builds owns operates and transfers (BOOT) the hydro power plant. The full requisites of the hydro power project contract are given below:

1. The production of the dam, canals and hydro power plant must be started by the contractor. The Government of MP will attain land which will submerge on creation of dam and must acclimatize the proprietors of land.

2. MCC must have right to run the hydro power project from date of commencement of commercial operations (DCCO) for a period of 20 years and must transfer the task to Government afterward. More, SPV must be tax released for a period of five years from DCCO viz. FY17-FY21.

3. The power project is of 600 megawatts (MW) must comprise 4 units of 150 MW each. The anticipated cost of project is approximately INR3, 500 Million to be spent over a period of 4 year(s) the project is anticipated to be commercially operational by April 1, 2016 with two units operational on same day and one unit each will be operational on April 1, 2017 and April 1, 2018.

4. Means of finance:

Means of Finance	INR Million
Government Aid (To be classified as Equity)	500
Equity	900
Debt	2100

Means of Finance INR Million
Government Aid (To be categorized as Equity) 500Equity 900
Debt 2100

5. Amount if expenses anticipated in various years is given below:

Cost of Project	INR Million		Debt	Funding Govt Aid	Equity	Total
FY13 (April to march)	700		0	250	450	700
FY14	1200		500	250	450	1200
FY15	1200		1200	-		1200
FY15	400		400	-		400

Debt must bear a fixed rate of interest of 10% and all interest till DCCO must be added to the principal. The anticipated principal beside with capitalized interest is anticipated to be INR2, 400 Million (viz.INR2100 Million debt plus INR300 Million capitalized interest). The reimbursement of the same must be in 12 equated yearly installments starting from FY17.

Short projections for the period of FY17 to FY21 are given

Particular	FY17	FY18	FY19	FY20	FY21
Revenue from Power sale	600	900	1200	1320	1452
EBITDA %	72%	68%	65%	60%	60%
Interest Cost	240.00	220.00	200.00	180.00	160.00
Depreciation	175.00	175.00	175.00	175.00	175.00
PAT	17.00	217.00	405.00	437.00	536.20

below:

Progresses as on March 31, 2015

The project manager for the SPV made given comments at a question and answer session on March 31, 2015:

Since everyone know, we were running bang on schedule till we last encountered on December 21, 2014. From this day we are just left with one more year to finish the task early enough. Still, the flash floods which effected our dam site on this March 15, 2015 have made chaos in the district. I must not emphasize the loss of lives in the district since everyone knows about that . Our project has also been seriously hit because of the same and we have been measuring the damage over the last one week. After examining damage, we have made changes in project schedule. Now we will be making just only one unit of 150 MW operational on April 1, 2016 and 1 unit each will be added in each of succeeding year(s).

Development as on September 30, 2015
Post the flash floods, lot of environmentalists started raising issues of changes in environment because of construction of huge number of dams. A few Public Interest Litigations (PILs) have been filed in various courts.

Honorable High Court of MP on September 27, 2015, restricted construction of any dams in the district and restricted authorizations for new dams till next hearing scheduled on November 30, 2015. MCC in its bulletin has specified that they will apply to the higher court on the issue.

After the progresses of March 31, 2015, supposing revenues are straightly related to the power production and the EBITDA margins stay intact for the year, as were projected, calculate the reviewed interest coverage ratio for FY17 and FY18?

A. FY17: 0.90; FY18: 1.85
B. FY17: 1.85; FY18: 2.93
C. FY17: 0.49; FY18: 0.97
D. FY17: 1.80; FY18: 2.78

QUESTION 3

Case Facts as on March 31, 2012

Mark Construction Company (MCC) obtained an agreement for construction of a huge dam and hydro power project on river Shivna in Madhya Pradesh (MP). The project is of significance from the irrigation perception because of its location and according to the contract MCC will have to start construction of web of canals, reach road to dam, power house and other auxiliary components. MCC is supported by Mr. Thomas Mark, member of parliament of a leading party which in recent times established government in MP. Traditionally, MCC has been involved with construction of rural roads, small bridges and railway stands on agreement basis for the Government. MCC will have a separate special purpose vehicle (SPV) presented for this project.

The hydro power project undergoes the public private partnership arrangement of the Government of MP, consequently the private partner builds owns operates and transfers (BOOT) the hydro power plant. The full requisites of the hydro power project contract are given below:

1. The production of the dam, canals and hydro power plant must be started by the contractor. The Government of MP will attain land which will submerge on creation of dam and must acclimatize the proprietors of land.

2. MCC must have right to run the hydro power project from date of commencement of commercial operations (DCCO) for a period of 20 years and must transfer the task to Government afterward. More, SPV must be tax released for a period of five years from DCCO viz. FY17-FY21.

3. The power project is of 600 megawatts (MW) must comprise 4 units of 150 MW each. The anticipated cost of project is approximately INR3, 500 Million to be spent over a period of 4 year(s) the project is anticipated to be commercially operational by April 1, 2016 with two units operational on same day and one unit each will be operational on April 1, 2017 and April 1, 2018.

4. Means of finance:

Means of Finance	INR Million
Government Aid (To be classified as Equity)	500
Equity	900
Debt	2100

Means of Finance INR Million
Government Aid (To be categorized as Equity) 500Equity 900
Debt 2100

5. Amount if expenses anticipated in various years is given below:

Cost of Project	INR Million		Funding Debt	Govt Aid	Equity	Total
FY13 (April to march)	700		0	250	450	700
FY14	1200		500	250	450	1200
FY15	1200		1200	-		1200
FY15	400		400	-		400

Debt must bear a fixed rate of interest of 10% and all interest till DCCO must be added to the principal. The anticipated principal beside with capitalized interest is anticipated to be INR2, 400 Million (viz.INR2100 Million debt plus INR300 Million capitalized interest). The reimbursement of the same must be in 12 equated yearly installments starting from FY17.

Short projections for the period of FY17 to FY21 are given

Particular	FY17	FY18	FY19	FY20	FY21
Revenue from Power sale	600	900	1200	1320	1452
EBITDA %	72%	68%	65%	60%	60%
Interest Cost	240.00	220.00	200.00	180.00	160.00
Depreciation	175.00	175.00	175.00	175.00	175.00
PAT	17.00	217.00	405.00	437.00	536.20

below:

Progresses as on March 31, 2015

The project manager for the SPV made given comments at a question and answer session on March 31, 2015:

Since everyone know, we were running bang on schedule till we last encountered on December 21, 2014. From this day we are just left with one more year to finish the task early enough. Still, the flash floods which effected our dam site on this March 15,

2015 have made chaos in the district. I must not emphasize the loss of lives in the district since everyone knows about that . Our project has also been seriously hit because of the same and we have been measuring the damage over the last one week. After examining damage, we have made changes in project schedule. Now we will be making just only one unit of 150 MW operational on April 1, 2016 and 1 unit each will be added in each of succeeding year(s).

Development as on September 30, 2015

Post the flash floods, lot of environmentalists started raising issues of changes in environment because of construction of huge number of dams. A few Public Interest Litigations (PILs) have been filed in various courts.

Honorable High Court of MP on September 27, 2015, restricted construction of any dams in the district and restricted authorizations for new dams till next hearing scheduled on November 30, 2015. MCC in its bulletin has specified that they will apply to the higher court on the issue.

As a credit rating expert on September 30, 2015, on receipt of the high court order, what rating action you will take:

A. Put ratings on rating watch.
B. Change rating outlook for long term to negative.
C. No action, wait for order if higher courts or hearing on November 30, 2015.
D. Instantly downgrade ratings of SPV.

QUESTION 4

Case Facts as on March 31, 2012

Mark Construction Company (MCC) obtained an agreement for construction of a huge dam and hydro power project on river Shivna in Madhya Pradesh (MP). The project is of significance from the irrigation perception because of its location and according to the contract MCC will have to start construction of web of canals, reach road to dam, power house and other auxiliary components. MCC is supported by Mr. Thomas Mark, member of parliament of a leading party which in recent times established government in MP. Traditionally, MCC has been involved with construction of rural roads, small bridges and railway stands on agreement basis for the Government. MCC will have a separate special purpose vehicle (SPV) presented for this project.

The hydro power project undergoes the public private partnership arrangement of the Government of MP, consequently the private partner builds owns operates and transfers (BOOT) the hydro power plant. The full requisites of the hydro power project contract are given below:

1. The production of the dam, canals and hydro power plant must be started by the contractor. The Government of MP will attain land which will submerge on creation of dam and must acclimatize the proprietors of land.

2. MCC must have right to run the hydro power project from date of commencement of commercial operations (DCCO) for a period of 20 years and must transfer the task to Government afterward. More, SPV must be tax released for a period of five years from DCCO viz. FY17-FY21.

3. The power project is of 600 megawatts (MW) must comprise 4 units of 150 MW each. The anticipated cost of project is approximately INR3, 500 Million to be spent over a period of 4 year(s) the project is anticipated to be commercially operational by April 1, 2016 with two units operational on same day and one unit each will be operational on April 1, 2017 and April 1, 2018.

4. Means of finance:

Means of Finance	INR Million
Government Aid (To be classified as Equity)	500
Equity	900
Debt	2100

Means of Finance INR Million
Government Aid (To be categorized as Equity) 500Equity 900
Debt 2100

5. Amount if expenses anticipated in various years is given below:

Cost of Project	INR Million		Funding			
		Debt	Govt Aid	Equity	Total
FY13 (April to march)	700	0	250	450	700
FY14	1200	500	250	450	1200
FY15	1200	1200	-		1200
FY15	400	400	-		400

Debt must bear a fixed rate of interest of 10% and all interest till DCCO must be added to the principal. The anticipated principal beside with capitalized interest is anticipated to be INR2, 400 Million (viz.INR2100 Million debt plus INR300 Million capitalized interest). The reimbursement of the same must be in 12 equated yearly installments starting from FY17.

Short projections for the period of FY17 to FY21 are given

Particular	FY17	FY18	FY19	FY20	FY21
Revenue from Power sale	600	900	1200	1320	1452
EBITDA %	72%	68%	65%	60%	60%
Interest Cost	240.00	220.00	200.00	180.00	160.00
Depreciation	175.00	175.00	175.00	175.00	175.00
PAT	17.00	217.00	405.00	437.00	536.20

below:

Progresses as on March 31, 2015

The project manager for the SPV made given comments at a question and answer session on March 31, 2015:

Since everyone know, we were running bang on schedule till we last encountered on December 21, 2014. From this day we are just left with one more year to finish the task early enough. Still, the flash floods which effected our dam site on this March 15, 2015 have made chaos in the district. I must not emphasize the loss of lives in the district since everyone knows about that . Our project has also been seriously hit because ofthe same and we have been measuring the damage over the last one week. After examining damage, we have made changes in project schedule. Now we will be making just only one unit of 150 MW operational on April 1, 2016 and 1 unit each will be added in each of succeeding year(s).

Development as on September 30, 2015
Post the flash floods, lot of environmentalists started raising issues of changes in environment because of construction of huge number of dams. A few Public Interest Litigations (PILs) have been filed in various courts.

Honorable High Court of MP on September 27, 2015, restricted construction of any dams in the district and restricted authorizations for new dams till next hearing scheduled on November 30, 2015. MCC in its bulletin has specified that they will apply to the higher court on the issue.

On receiving the credit proposal, the banker notified the company that in FY17 the DSCR is below unity, which is not acceptable to bank. Which of the given is precise?

A. Had the cash accruals be more by INR50 Million, DSCR would have been unity. SPV can offer an implicit credit improvement for the same from MCC.
B. Had the cash accruals be more by INR8 Million, DSCR would have been unity. SPV can offer an implicit credit improvement for the same from MCC.
C. Had the cash accruals be more by INR8 Million, DSCR would have been unity, SPV can offer an explicit credit improvement for the same from MCC.
D. Had the cash accruals be more by INR12 Million, DSCR would have been unity. SPV can offer an explicit credit improvement for the same from MCC.

QUESTION 5

Blake is a credit expert with a credit rating organization in India. He was examining Oil and Gas Industry corporations and has

Particulars	A Ltd	B Ltd	C Ltd	D Ltd
Total Income	2000	2400	3000	3500
EBITDA	500	550	650	460
Interest	100	100	125	130
Total Debt	1000	1400	1000	1500

displayed short financials for given 4 entities:

Two credit experts are talking over the DM-approach to credit danger modeling. They make the given declarations:

Expert A: A case's standard deviation of credit losses can be decided by considering the standard deviation of credit losses of individual exposures in the case and summarizing it up.

Expert B: I do not completely approve with that. Aside from individual standard deviations, one should also needs to consider the correlation of the exposure with the rest of the case so as to account for modification effects. Higher correlations amongst credit exposures will set in motion higher standard deviation of the general case.

A. Just only Expert A is precise
B. Each are precise
C. Just only Expert B is precise
D. Each are wrong

QUESTION 6

Blake is a credit expert with a credit rating organization in India. He was examining Oil and Gas Industry corporations and has

Particulars	A Ltd	B Ltd	C Ltd	D Ltd
Total Income	2000	2400	3000	3500
EBITDA	500	550	650	460
Interest	100	100	125	130
Total Debt	1000	1400	1000	1500

displayed short financials for given 4 entities:

Giving equal weightage to all three ratios, decide which of these entities must be rated highest on a relative scale.

A. C Ltd
B. A Ltd
C. D Ltd
D. B Ltd

QUESTION 7

Blake is a credit expert with a credit rating organization in India. He was examining Oil and Gas Industry corporations and has

Particulars	A Ltd	B Ltd	C Ltd	D Ltd
Total Income	2000	2400	3000	3500
EBITDA	500	550	650	460
Interest	100	100	125	130
Total Debt	1000	1400	1000	1500

displayed short financials for given 4 entities:

Which of the given reports is wrong?

A. B Ltd has higher EBITDA margins in comparison with C Ltd.
B. D Ltd has higher EBITDA margins in comparison with B Ltd.
C. C Ltd has poorest total debt to EBITDA ratio.
D. B Ltd has poorest interest coverage ratio.

QUESTION 8

Given is data related banks:

Auckland Ltd is a public sector bank in service with approximately 120 branches across India. The bank has been in business since 1971 and has approximately 40% branches in rural areas and approximately 75% of all branches are in Western India. Based on the size, Auckland Ltd will be graded at number 31 between 40 banks in India.
Even if top management has employment period of 5 years, mostly they retire on ach sieving age of 60 years with an average tenure of just only 2 years at the top job.

Profit and Loss Account

Particulars	FY11	FY12	FY13
Interest on advances bills	124,000	182.000	283,000
Interest on investments	15,000	18,000	14,000
Interest on balances with Banking Regulator and other inter-bank funds	1, 100	1,000	1,700
Other interest income	40,000	49,000	54,000
Other Income	80,000	95,000	99,000
Total Income	260,100	345,000	451,700
Interest expenses	105,000	148,000	235,000
Operating expenses	23,000	28,000	32,000
Total expenditure	128,000	176,000	267,000
Operating Profit	155,100	197,000	216,700
Provisions	72,000	102,000	174,000
Profit before tax	83,100	95,000	42,700
Tax	16,600	19,000	8,500
Profit after Tax	66,500	76,000	34,200

Balance Sheet

Assets	March 31 2011	March 31 2012	March 31 2013
Cash and Balances with Reserve Bank of India	120,000	420,000	770,000
Balances with Banks and Money at Call and Short Notice	745,000	789,000	1194,000
Investments	598,000	689,000	1139,000
Advances	1432,000	1709,000	2485,000
Fixed Assets	223,000	234,000	245,000
Other Assets	567,000	670,000	970,000
TOTAL	3685,000	4511,000	6803,000

Liabilities	March 31 2011	March 31 2012	March 31 2013
Capital	31,000	31,000	42,000
Reserves and Surplus	294,000	370,000	1154,000
Deposits	2100,000	2120,000	2450,000
Borrowings	960,000	1590,000	2657,000
Other Liabilities and Provisions	300,000	400,000	500,000
TOTAL	3685,000	4511,000	6803,000

The rating wise break-up of assets for FY11 is given below:

Rating	FY11
AAA	120,000
AA	530,000
A	220,000
BBB	150,000
BB and below	310,000
Unrated	102,000
Total	1432,000

The core spreads for FY13 in comparison with FY12 have:

A. Expanded by 136 bps
B. Shrank by 327 bps
C. Shrank by 136 bps
D. Expanded by 191 bps

QUESTION 9

Given is data related banks:

Auckland Ltd is a public sector bank in service with approximately 120 branches across India. The bank has been in business since 1971 and has approximately 40% branches in rural areas and approximately 75% of all branches are in Western India. Based on the size, Auckland Ltd will be graded at number 31 between 40 banks in India.
Even if top management has employment period of 5 years, mostly they retire on ach sieving age of 60 years with an average tenure of just only 2 years at the top job.

Profit and Loss Account

Particulars	FY11	FY12	FY13
Interest on advances bills	124,000	182.000	283,000
Interest on investments	15,000	18,000	14,000
Interest on balances with Banking Regulator and other inter-bank funds	1, 100	1,000	1,700
Other interest income	40,000	49,000	54,000
Other Income	80,000	95,000	99,000
Total Income	260,100	345,000	451,700
Interest expenses	105,000	148,000	235,000
Operating expenses	23,000	28,000	32,000
Total expenditure	128,000	176,000	267,000
Operating Profit	155,100	197,000	216,700
Provisions	72,000	102,000	174,000
Profit before tax	83,100	95,000	42,700
Tax	16,600	19,000	8,500
Profit after Tax	66,500	76,000	34,200

Balance Sheet

Assets	March 31 2011	March 31 2012	March 31 2013
Cash and Balances with Reserve Bank of India	120,000	420,000	770,000
Balances with Banks and Money at Call and Short Notice	745,000	789,000	1194,000
Investments	598,000	689,000	1139,000
Advances	1432,000	1709,000	2485,000
Fixed Assets	223,000	234,000	245,000
Other Assets	567,000	670,000	970,000
TOTAL	3685,000	4511,000	6803,000

Liabilities	March 31 2011	March 31 2012	March 31 2013
Capital	31,000	31,000	42,000
Reserves and Surplus	294,000	370,000	1154,000
Deposits	2100,000	2120,000	2450,000
Borrowings	960,000	1590,000	2657,000
Other Liabilities and Provisions	300,000	400,000	500,000
TOTAL	3685,000	4511,000	6803,000

The rating wise break-up of assets for FY11 is given below:

Rating	FY11
AAA	120,000
AA	530,000
A	220,000
BBB	150,000
BB and below	310,000
Unrated	102,000
Total	1432,000

The ROTA for Auckland declined from___in FY12 to__in FY13.

A. 0,.7%, 0,3%
B. 7%; 2%
C. 2.3%; 0.7%
D. 1.9%; 0.6%

QUESTION 10

Given is data related banks:

Auckland Ltd is a public sector bank in service with approximately 120 branches across India. The bank has been in business since 1971 and has approximately 40% branches in rural areas and approximately 75% of all branches are in Western India. Based on the size, Auckland Ltd will be graded at number 31 between 40 banks in India.
Even if top management has employment period of 5 years, mostly they retire on ach sieving age of 60 years with an average tenure of just only 2 years at the top job.

Profit and Loss Account

Particulars	FY11	FY12	FY13
Interest on advances bills	124,000	182.000	283,000
Interest on investments	15,000	18,000	14,000
Interest on balances with Banking Regulator and other inter-bank funds	1, 100	1,000	1,700
Other interest income	40,000	49,000	54,000
Other Income	80,000	95,000	99,000
Total Income	260,100	345,000	451,700
Interest expenses	105,000	148,000	235,000
Operating expenses	23,000	28,000	32,000
Total expenditure	128,000	176,000	267,000
Operating Profit	155,100	197,000	216,700
Provisions	72,000	102,000	174,000
Profit before tax	83,100	95,000	42,700
Tax	16,600	19,000	8,500
Profit after Tax	66,500	76,000	34,200

Balance Sheet

Assets	March 31 2011	March 31 2012	March 31 2013
Cash and Balances with Reserve Bank of India	120,000	420,000	770,000
Balances with Banks and Money at Call and Short Notice	745,000	789,000	1194,000
Investments	598,000	689,000	1139,000
Advances	1432,000	1709,000	2485,000
Fixed Assets	223,000	234,000	245,000
Other Assets	567,000	670,000	970,000
TOTAL	3685,000	4511,000	6803,000

Liabilities	March 31 2011	March 31 2012	March 31 2013
Capital	31,000	31,000	42,000
Reserves and Surplus	294,000	370,000	1154,000
Deposits	2100,000	2120,000	2450,000
Borrowings	960,000	1590,000	2657,000
Other Liabilities and Provisions	300,000	400,000	500,000
TOTAL	3685,000	4511,000	6803,000

The rating wise break-up of assets for FY11 is given below:

Rating	FY11
AAA	120,000
AA	530,000
A	220,000
BBB	150,000
BB and below	310,000
Unrated	102,000
Total	1432,000

Cost to income ratio is best for which year

A. FY13
B. FY11
C. Same FY11 and FY12
D. FY12

QUESTION 11

Given is data related banks:

Auckland Ltd is a public sector bank in service with approximately 120 branches across India. The bank has been in business since 1971 and has approximately 40% branches in rural areas and approximately 75% of all branches are in Western India. Based on the size, Auckland Ltd will be graded at number 31 between 40 banks in India.
Even if top management has employment period of 5 years, mostly they retire on ach sieving age of 60 years with an average tenure of just only 2 years at the top job.

Profit and Loss Account

Particulars	FY11	FY12	FY13
Interest on advances bills	124,000	182.000	283,000
Interest on investments	15,000	18,000	14,000
Interest on balances with Banking Regulator and other inter-bank funds	1, 100	1,000	1,700
Other interest income	40,000	49,000	54,000
Other Income	80,000	95,000	99,000
Total Income	260,100	345,000	451,700
Interest expenses	105,000	148,000	235,000
Operating expenses	23,000	28,000	32,000
Total expenditure	128,000	176,000	267,000
Operating Profit	155,100	197,000	216,700
Provisions	72,000	102,000	174,000
Profit before tax	83,100	95,000	42,700
Tax	16,600	19,000	8,500
Profit after Tax	66,500	76,000	34,200

Balance Sheet

Assets	March 31 2011	March 31 2012	March 31 2013
Cash and Balances with Reserve Bank of India	120,000	420,000	770,000
Balances with Banks and Money at Call and Short Notice	745,000	789,000	1194,000
Investments	598,000	689,000	1139,000
Advances	1432,000	1709,000	2485,000
Fixed Assets	223,000	234,000	245,000
Other Assets	567,000	670,000	970,000
TOTAL	3685,000	4511,000	6803,000

Liabilities	March 31 2011	March 31 2012	March 31 2013
Capital	31,000	31,000	42,000
Reserves and Surplus	294,000	370,000	1154,000
Deposits	2100,000	2120,000	2450,000
Borrowings	960,000	1590,000	2657,000
Other Liabilities and Provisions	300,000	400,000	500,000
TOTAL	3685,000	4511,000	6803,000

The rating wise break-up of assets for FY11 is given below:

Rating	FY11
AAA	120,000
AA	530,000
A	220,000
BBB	150,000
BB and below	310,000
Unrated	102,000
Total	1432,000

Computer danger subjective assets for Auckland Ltd for FY11:

A. 10,10,000 Million
B. 13,24,500 Million
C. 11,64,500 Million
D. 11,60,000 Million

QUESTION 12

Ms. Karen Smith is a credit rating expert. She organized a full report about one of her customer, FlyHigh Airlines Ltd, a corporation operating chartered aircrafts in India. As she was going for a meeting with her boss on the issue, tea spilled on her set of organized documents. Since she was late for meeting, as an alternative of organizing whole set she could recall some numbers from her memory and reassembled given partial

Period Ended	FY10	FY11	FY12
Working Results			
Total Income			
EBITDA			
Interest			
Depreciation	20.00	25.00	30.00
Effective Tax Rate	20%	24%	25%
PBT			
PAT			
Financial Position			
Net Worth	370.00	430.00	535.67
Total Debt	743.00		
Ratios			
Growth			
Growth in Total Income (%)		25%	15%
Growth in EBITDA (%)		30%	20%
Growth in PAT (%)		20%	
Profitability			
EBITDA Margins		32%	
PAT Margins			
RONW			
Solvency			
Overall Gearing Ratio		2.2	
Interest coverage ratio	3.2		3.1
Total Debt / EBITDA		4.5	5.2

financial table:

What is Total Income FY10 and FY12?

A. FY10: INR400 Million; FY12:INR575 Million
B. FY10: INR525.56 Million; FY12: INR755.49 Million
C. Inadequate Data to calculate
D. FY10: INR656.94 Million; FY12: INR821.18 Million

QUESTION 13

Ms. Karen Smith is a credit rating expert. She organized a full report about one of her customer, FlyHigh Airlines Ltd, a corporation operating chartered aircrafts in India. As she was going for a meeting with her boss on the issue, tea spilled over her set of organized documents. Since she was late for meeting, as an alternative of organizing whole set she could recall few numbers from her memory and reassembled given partial financial table:

Period Ended	FY10	FY11	FY12
Working Results			
Total Income			
EBITDA			
Interest			
Depreciation	20.00	25.00	30.00
Effective Tax Rate	20%	24%	25%
PBT			
PAT			
Financial Position			
Net Worth	370.00	430.00	535.67
Total Debt	743.00		
Ratios			
Growth			
Growth in Total Income (%)		25%	15%
Growth in EBITDA (%)		30%	20%
Growth in PAT (%)		20%	
Profitability			
EBITDA Margins		32%	
PAT Margins			
RONW			
Solvency			
Overall Gearing Ratio		2.2	
Interest coverage ratio	3.2		3.1
Total Debt / EBITDA		4.5	5.2

Calculate Interest for FY10 and FY12?

A. Inadequate Data to calculate
B. FY10: INR50.53 Million; FY12:INR81.38 Million

C. FY10: INR161.71 Million; FY12: INR252.27 Million
D. FY10: INR17.47 Million; FY12:INR782.03 Million

QUESTION 14

Liam Mason, an expert fixed income trader is leading interviews for the job of a subordinate fixed income trader. He interviewed four applicants Logan, Nathan, Donna and Robert and given are the answers to his questions.

Question 1: Tell a little regarding Option Adjusted Spread

Logan: OAS is valid just only to bond which do not have any options connected to it. It is for the plain bonds.

Nathan: In bonds with fixed options, AS reveals not just only the credit danger but also reveals prepayment danger over and above the Standard.

Donna: Since spreads are calculated to identify the level of credit danger in the bound, OAS is difference among in the Z spread and price of a call option for a callable bond.

Robert: For callable bond OAS will be lower than Z Spread.

Question 2: This is a spread that need to be added to the Standard zero rate curve in a parallel shift so that the sum of the dangerous bond's discounted cash flows equals its existing market price. Which Spread I am talking on the subject of?

Logan: Z Spread Nathan: Nominal Spread
Donna: Option Adjusted Spread Robert: Asset Swap Spread

Question 3: What do you know on the subject of Interpolated spread and yield spread?

Logan: Yield spread is the difference among the YTM of a dangerous bond and the YTM of an on-the-run treasury Standard bond whose maturity is closest, but not similar to that of dangerous bond. Interpolated spread is the spread among the YTM of dangerous bond and the YTM of same maturity treasury Standard, which is interpolated from the two nearest on-the-run treasury securities.

Nathan: Interpolated spread is chosen to yield spread for the reason that the latter has the maturity mismatch, which leads to error if the yield curve is not flat and the Standard security changes over time, leading to discrepancy.

Donna: Interpolated spread takes account the shape of the Standard yield curve and so better than yield spread.
Robert: Each Interpolated Spread and Yield Spread rely on YTM which suffers from disadvantages and irregularities for example the supposition of flat yield curve and reinvestment at YTM itself.

Then Liam gave given data related to the Standard YTMs:

Maturity(yrs)	1	2	3	4	5
YTM	8.22	8.52	8.88	8.98	9.02

There is an 8.75% dangerous bond with a maturity of 2.75% year(s). Its existing price is INR102.31, which matches to YTM of 8.52%. Calculate Yield Spread from the data offered in the illustration:

A. 0.13%
B. 0.00%
C. 0.36%
D. 0.27%

QUESTION 15

The given data relates to bonds:

Bond	Initial Maturity	Spread from G-Sec (bps)		
		January 2013	April 2013	July 2013
Bond A	10 Years	94	97	89
Bond B	10 Years	102	103	93
Bond C	10 Years	370	530	560
Bond D	10 Years	115	130	110
Bond E	10 Years	10	15	7

More given data is obtainable regarding a particular bond 'Bond F'

There is a 10.25% dangerous bond with a maturity of 2.25% year(s) its existing price is INR105.31, which matches to YTM of 9.22%. The given are the Standard YTMs.

Maturity(yrs)	1	2	3	4	5
YTM	8.22	8.52	8.88	8.98	9.02

From the time January 2013 to April 2013, what can you expect on the subject of the market conditions, assuming the G-Sec has not changed?

A. There has been credit spread compression, which means the spreads have declined, which can be lead indicator of oncoming economy stress.

B. There has been widening of credit spread, which means the spreads have increased, which can be lead indicator of oncoming economy stress.

C. There has been widening of credit spread, which means the spreads have increased, which can be lead indicator of oncoming economy stress.

D. There has been credit spread compression, which means the spreads have declines, which can be lead indicator of oncoming economy boom.

QUESTION 16

The given data relates to bonds:

Bond	Initial Maturity	Spread from G-Sec (bps)		
		January 2013	April 2013	July 2013
Bond A	10 Years	94	97	89
Bond B	10 Years	102	103	93
Bond C	10 Years	370	530	560
Bond D	10 Years	115	130	110
Bond E	10 Years	10	15	7

More given data is available concerning a particular bond 'Bond F'

There is a 10.25% dangerous bond with a maturity of 2.25% year(s) its existing price is INR105.31, which matches to YTM of 9.22%. The given are the Standard YTMs.

Maturity(yrs)	1	2	3	4	5
YTM	8.22	8.52	8.88	8.98	9.02

Given are the significance of Industry Analysis:

Report 1: Evaluating Industry danger is the first and foremost step for top down approach of analysis.

Report 2: Industry Analysis is appropriate for examining the

industry life cycle, which is highly essential from the perception of

an investor or lender. State which is/are precise?

A. Each are wrong
B. Each are precise
C. Just only Report 2 is precise
D. Just only Report 1 is precise

QUESTION 17

If ABC Ltd. acquires (with acquisition and installation of machinery) using cash, which of the given ratios will stay unchanged, if all other things remain persistent?

A. None of the three
B. Asset Turnover ratio
C. Existing Ratio
D. Quick Ratio

QUESTION 18

Mr. Gabe, while teaching the CCRA lesson to pupils defined Altman's Model and specified that given variables do occur for Altman's Model:

1. total debt/total assets,
2. retained earnings/total assets.
3. earnings before interest and taxes/total assets,
4. market value equity/book value of total liabilities,
5. sales/total assets

Precisely how many variables are wrongly identified?

A. Precisely Four
B. Precisely One
C. Precisely Two
D. Precisely Three

QUESTION 19

In Steepening short term rates____relative to long term rate

A. decreases
B. increases
C. is autonomous of each other
D. stays determined

QUESTION 20

If you yield curve is humped and the medium rates drop, what will happen to the yield curve?

A. It will move from negative to positive
B. It will shift up in a uniform fashion
C. It will become steeper
D. It will flatten

QUESTION 21

Which of the given report is inaccurate?

A. DEF Ltd. has received a speculative grade rating as its excellent rating is B+
B. Non-Convertible debenture of PQR Ltd. has a speculative rating since its excellent rating is C
C. ABC Ltd. short term is BBB- for its commercial paper
D. ABC has an investment grade rating as his excellent rating is A1

QUESTION 22

Which of the given is not one of the C in the 5 C Model?

A. Capacity
B. Capital
C. Covenants
D. Conditions

QUESTION 23

Z spreads in Callable bonds comprise:

A. Does not comprise premium for credit danger and call option price for prepayment danger.
B. Premium for credit danger and call option price for prepayment danger in comprised.
C. Premium for credit danger is just only comprised.
D. Premium for call option price for prepayment danger is just only comprised.

QUESTION 24

Danger in CDS price is reflective of

A. rise in probability of default

B. rise in interest rates
C. fall in probability of default
D. rise in recovery rates

QUESTION 25

Which of the given is a factor considered while evaluating resources profile for rating of bank?

A. Size and growth of deposits
B. All of the three
C. Deposit composition & stickiness
D. Geographic distribution of deposits

QUESTION 26

Which of the given are kinds of bank guarantee?

A. Deferred and Term
B. Financial and Performance
C. Stance and Sight

QUESTION 27

Mr. A shares details of two bonds given below:

Particulars	Bond X	Bond Y
Yeild to Maturity	7%	9%
Maturity	2.25 Years	4.75 years
Number of coupons in the year	1	1

Term Structure:

1 Year	6.8%
2 Year	7.2%
3 Year	7.8%
4 Year	8.6%
5 Year	9.2%
6 Year	9.9%

Conclude the interpolated spread for Bond X and Bond Y?

A. Bond X: 80 bps Bond Y: Negative
B. Bond X: 35 bps Bond Y: 5 bps
C. Bond X: 65 bps Bond Y: Nil
D. Bond X: 20 bps Bond Y: 20 bps

QUESTION 28

Attributes of healthy cultural values eliminate:

A. Experienced management.
B. Diversified sources of revenue.
C. Brand.
D. Healthy relationship with workers

QUESTION 29

For considering the assignment of probabilities, which of the given characteristics are taken into account?

A. Economic cycle – bearish phase or boom
B. All of the other options
C. The date of valuation of assets on the financials
D. The nature and age of assets

QUESTION 30

Project 1: Corporation X has a sugar mill at Philadelphia and is replicating same at Toronto.
Project 2: Corporation Y has a sugar mill at Philadelphia and is

rising capacity from 100000 MT to 140000 MT per annum. What

kind of projects are Project 1 and Project 2?

A. Project 1: Modification; Project 2: Forward Integration
B. Project 1: Expansion; Project 2: Forward Integration
C. Project 1: Modification; Project 2: Expansion
D. Project 1: Expansion; Project 2: Expansion

QUESTION 31

Which of the given may set in motion the worsening in credit profile of a bank?

Report 1. Bank's Capital adequacy falling below regulatory requirement. Report 2. Rise in Slippage ratio

A. None of the report is precise
B. Each report 1 and 2 are precise
C. Report 1 is precise
D. Report 2 is precise

QUESTION 32

Which of the given reports concerning having a CEO serve as chairman of the board is most accurate? Having a CEO also serve as chairman is considered:

A. poor corporate governance practice as having the CEO server as chairman is an inherent conflict when determining management compensation.
B. good corporate governance practice as the CEO is the best individual to offer the board with data on the subject of the company's strategy and operations.
C. cannot be decided
D. poor corporate governance practice as having the CEO and chairman serve as separate positions ensures a properly-functioning board.

QUESTION 33

A holder of which of the given kinds of bonds is minimum likely to undergo from rising interest rates?

A. Floating rate bonds
B. Fixed rate bond
C. Zero-coupon bonds

QUESTION 34

The most essential metric for a bank is the Net Interest Income (NII) which is the difference among_____income and_____expense.

A. Interest; Total
B. Interest; Fee
C. Interest; Interest
D. Total; Total

QUESTION 35

Based on the normal size report analysis which of the given report regarding worker cost is precise?

Particulars (USD Million)	YE FY14	YE FY15
SALES	2800	3800
Employee Cost	1200	1400
Power and Establishment Cost	160	180
Depreciation	26	31
Interest	25	37
Taxes	200	240

A. The worker cost is anticipated to contribute 8% to fall in PAT in FY15
B. The worker cost is anticipated to contribute 7% to fall in PAT in FY15
C. The worker cost is anticipated to contribute 6% to fall in PAT in FY15
D. The worker cost is anticipated to contribute 5% to fall in PAT in FY15

QUESTION 36

Butterfly strategy is a combination of

A. Ladder and Barbell on the same market sides
B. Barbell and Bullet on the opposite market sides
C. Barbell and Bullet on the same market sides
D. Ladder and barbell on the opposite market sides

QUESTION 37

Awesome Mobile Ltd is a leading mobile seller who manufactures mobile phone under own brand Awesome. Which of the given is the biggest commercial danger for Awesome?

A. Technology Danger
B. Branding danger
C. Raw material price danger
D. Competition

QUESTION 38

Based on the Moody's KMV model which of the given is not precise?

A: Growth variables are essential for default analysis. rapid growth will set in motion lower probability of default and rapid decline will set in motion higher probability of default. B: Activity ratios are appropriate for default analysis. A huge stock of inventories relative to sales will set in motion a higher probability of default.

A. Just only Report A is precise
B. Each the reports are precise
C. None of the reports is precise
D. Just only Report B is precise

QUESTION 39

In a failing economy, which of the given is least accurate?

A. Interest costs go up and create refunding danger for those who have bonds maturing which need to be rolled over.
B. Interest costs go up and create rate danger for have bonds maturing which need to be rolled over.
C. None of the other options.
D. Interest costs go up and create funding danger for those who have borrowing plans lined up.

QUESTION 40

Which of the given is not an importance of the sovereign rating?

A: To reach at cost of lending to a country
B: To set lower floor for the rating of the corporate and banks of the countries on global scale. C: For deciding the danger levels for international investment cases

A. Just only A and C
B. Just only B
C. Just only A and B
D. None of the three

QUESTION 41

Stand by letter of credits are characteristically taken as credit improvement for_____

A. Commercial Paper
B. Long term Bond issues
C. Long term debenture issues
D. Bank debt

QUESTION 42

Report 1: The Yields on the MBS PTCs are normally higher than the yields on the corporate bonds of similar ratings.
Report 2: The reason for alteration in yields on the corporate bonds and correspondingly rated PTCs is on account of the optionality in the PTC, the unfamiliarity of the structure and doubts in respect of legal and structural issues.

Which of the above reports is precise?

A. None of the reports
B. Each the reports
C. Just only Report 2 is precise
D. Just only Report 1 is precise

QUESTION 43

Which of the given is NOT a conceptual definition of credit danger on which credit models are based?

A. Default Mode Paradigm
B. Value-at-Danger paradigm
C. Mark-to-Market Paradigm

QUESTION 44

Which of the given is inaccurate in case of credit improvements?

A. It lessens the default danger of the borrowing entity for the lender, thereby deteriorating the general credit worthiness of the borrower
B. Credit improvement could be implicit or explicit
C. Credit improvement is a mechanism whereby external cash flows is extended by an entity which has a stringer credit profile, so that it benefits the fund raising entity

QUESTION 45

Short term rates are decided by_____

A. All of the other options
B. Liquidity position caused by seasonal demand supply for credit
C. Foreign case investment inflows and outflows
D. Bunching of tax and government payments

QUESTION 46

Which of the given factor is considered while undertaking management evaluation?

A. All of the other options
B. Corporate Strategy
C. Performance of group concerns
D. Past track record

QUESTION 47

_____Strategy entails of buying a bond with maturity longer than the investment horizon (for investor) or buying a long-maturity bond with short-term funding through repo (for speculator).

A. Barbell, Ladder and Butterfly
B. Yield Spread Anticipation
C. Rate Anticipation with Maturity Mismatch
D. Riding the yield curve

ANSWER

1. Correct Answer: C
2. Correct Answer: B
3. Correct Answer: A
4. Correct Answer: C
5. Correct Answer: C
6. Correct Answer: C
7. Correct Answer: A
8. Correct Answer: C
9. Correct Answer: C
10. Correct Answer: A
11. Correct Answer: C
12. Correct Answer: A
13. Correct Answer: C
14. Correct Answer: C
15. Correct Answer: C
16. Correct Answer: B
17. Correct Answer: C
18. Correct Answer: A
    Reference:
    https://www.investopedia.com/terms/a/altman.asp
19. Correct Answer: A
    Reference:
    https://www.analystforum.com/forums/cfa-
    forums/cfa-level-ii-forum/91348766
20. Correct Answer: C
21. Correct Answer: B
22. Correct Answer: C
    Reference:
    https://www.investopedia.com/terms/f/five-c-
    credit.asp
23. Correct Answer: B
    Reference:
    https://books.google.com.pk/books?id=WTvNAgAA

QBAJ&pg=PA224&lpg=PA224&dq=credit+Z+spread
s+in+Callable+bonds+include+Premium+for+credit+
risk+and+call+option+price+for+prepayment+risk+i
n+included&source=bl&ots=cdWVJiWQSC&sig=d9Y
2vg5dylZlrlBT7tmKRihUg2M&hl=en&sa=X&ved=2ah
UKEwiUqN2l_93eAhXMA8AKHSb1B7gQ6AEwCXoE
CAcQ
AQ#v=onepage&q=credit%20Z%20spreads%20in%2
0Callable%20bonds%20include%20Premium%20for
%20credit%20risk%20and%20call%20option%20pric
e%
20for%20prepayment%20risk%20in%20included&f=f
alse
24. Correct Answer: A
25. Correct Answer: B
26. Correct Answer: B
    Reference https://www.hdfcbank.com/sme/trade-services/letters-of-credit-and-bank-guarantees
27. Correct Answer: B
28. Correct Answer: B
29. Correct Answer: C
30. Correct Answer: C
31. Correct Answer: B
32. Correct Answer: D
33. Correct Answer: A
    Reference: https://www.nuveen.com/fixed-income-strategies-for-low-and-rising-rates
34. Correct Answer: C
    Reference:
    https://economictimes.indiatimes.com/definition/net-interest-income-nii
35. Correct Answer: C
36. Correct Answer: B
    Reference:
    https://books.google.com.pk/books?id=WTvNAgAA
    QBAJ&pg=PA213&lpg=PA213&dq=Butterfly+strateg
    y+is+a+combination+of+Barbell+and+Bullet+on+the
    +opposite+market+sides&source=bl&ots=cdWVJkV

MRG&sig=XIB-
7YqySq5YDEUmEWusH5JCsjY&hl=en&sa=X&ved=2
ahUKEwj3_pCrxN7eAhVkK8AKHYuDCwUQ6AEwBn
oECAUQAQ#v=onepage&q=Butterfly%20strategy%2
0is%20a%20combination%20of%20Barbell%20and%
20Bullet%20on%20the%20opposite%20market%20si
des&f=false

37. **Correct Answer: C**
38. **Correct Answer: D**
   Reference:
   https://books.google.com.pk/books?id=g8XgCwAA
   QBAJ&pg=PA67&lpg=PA67&dq=Activity+ratios+are
   +relevant+for+default+analysis.+A+large+stock+of+i
   nventories+relative+to+sales+will+lead+to+a+higher
   +probability+of+default&source=bl&ots=Q-
   6qbboNbl&sig=iKGUJsn0wKNSv-
   F7pZ5B_GEIw5E&hl=en&sa=X&ved=2ahUKEwjsruK
   Zwd7eAhUqB8AKHQFGAtAQ6AEwC3oECAsQAQ#v
   =onepage&q=Activity%20ratios%20are%20relevant
   %
   20for%20default%20analysis.%20A%20large%20sto
   ck%20of%20inventories%20relative%20to%20sales
   %20will%20lead%20to%20a%20higher%20probabilit
   y% 20of%20default&f=false
39. **Correct Answer: D**
40. **Correct Answer: B**
41. **Correct Answer: D**
   Reference:
   https://www.investopedia.com/terms/s/standbyletter
   ofcredit.asp
42. **Correct Answer: D**
   Reference:
   https://books.google.com.pk/books?id=WTvNAgAA
   QBAJ&pg=PA305&lpg=PA305&dq=The+Yields+on+t
   he+MBS+PTCs+are+normally+higher+than+the+yiel
   ds+on+the+corporate+bonds+of+similar+ratings&s
   ource=bl&ots=cdWVJkUPUC&sig=LXN-
   pawMofH61opTbPnHkHoNc0l&hl=en&sa=X&ved=2a

hUKEwiSldjpwd7eAhUMDsAKHbneBtsQ6AEwAHoE
CAkQAQ#v=onepage&q=The%20Yields%20on%20th
e%
20MBS%20PTCs%20are%20normally%20higher%20
than%20the%20yields%20on%20the%20corporate%
20bonds%20of%20similar%20ratings&f=false

43. Correct Answer: B
    Reference:
    http://www.bulentsenver.com/yeditepe/pdf/Credit%2
    0Risk%20Modelling%20BIS49.pdf (page 9)
44. Correct Answer: A
45. Correct Answer: A
46. Correct Answer: D
47. Correct Answer: D
    Reference:
    https://books.google.com.pk/books?id=WTvNAgAA
    QBAJ&pg=PA276&lpg=PA276&dq=Strategy+consist
    s+of+buying+a+bond+with+maturity+longer+than+t
    he+investment+horizon+(for+investor)+or+buying+a
    +long-maturity+bond+with+short-
    term+funding+through+repo&source=bl&ots=cdWV
    JkURVE&sig=zdil1Gm3sNJnB6zDJ82O-
    kMAAtk&hl=en&sa=X&ved=2ahUKEwiYoNDOwt7eA
    hUFDsAKHWG8BvcQ6AEwAHoECAkQAQ#v=onepa
    ge&q=Strategy%20consists%20of%20buying%20a%
    20bond%20with%20maturity%20longer%20than%20
    the%20investment%20horizon%20(for%20investor)
    %20or%20buying%20a%20long-
    maturity%20bond%20wit%20short-
    term%20funding%20through%20repo&f=false

www.ingramcontent.com/pod-product-compliance
Lightning Source LLC
LaVergne TN
LVHW051623050326
832903LV00033B/4636